Dramatic Debuts
Volume 5

A Study of Limits
Emily Sheera Cutler

**Entropy Increasing
in a Closed System**
Justin Krasner-Karpen

Forsooth!
Connor Foley

A Samuel French Acting Edition

SAMUELFRENCH.COM
SAMUELFRENCH-LONDON.CO.UK

A STUDY OF LIMITS Copyright © 2014 by Emily Sheera Cutler
ENTROPY INCREASING IN A CLOSED SYSTEM Copyright © 2014 by Justin Krasner-Karpen
FORSOOTH! Copyright © 2014 by Connor M. Foley
All Rights Reserved

A STUDY OF LIMITS, ENTROPY INCREASING IN A CLOSED SYSTEM, and *FORSOOTH* is fully protected under the copyright laws of the United States of America, the British Commonwealth, including Canada, and all other countries of the Copyright Union. All rights, including professional and amateur stage productions, recitation, lecturing, public reading, motion picture, radio broadcasting, television and the rights of translation into foreign languages are strictly reserved.

ISBN 978-0-573-70209-9

www.SamuelFrench.com
www.SamuelFrench-London.co.uk

For Production Enquiries

United States and Canada
Info@SamuelFrench.com
1-866-598-8449

United Kingdom and Europe
Plays@SamuelFrench-London.co.uk
020-7255-4302

Each title is subject to availability from Samuel French, depending upon country of performance. Please be aware that *A STUDY OF LIMITS, ENTROPY INCREASING IN A CLOSED SYSTEM,* and *FORSOOTH* may not be licensed by Samuel French in your territory. Professional and amateur producers should contact the nearest Samuel French office or licensing partner to verify availability.

CAUTION: Professional and amateur producers are hereby warned that *A STUDY OF LIMITS, ENTROPY INCREASING IN A CLOSED SYSTEM*, and *FORSOOTH* is subject to a licensing fee. Publication of this play(s) does not imply availability for performance. Both amateurs and professionals considering a production are strongly advised to apply to Samuel French before starting rehearsals, advertising, or booking a theatre. A licensing fee must be paid whether the title(s) is presented for charity or gain and whether or not admission is charged. Professional/Stock licensing fees are quoted upon application to Samuel French.

No one shall make any changes in this title(s) for the purpose of production. No part of this book may be reproduced, stored in a retrieval system, or transmitted in any form, by any means, now known or yet to be invented, including mechanical, electronic, photocopying, recording, videotaping, or otherwise, without the prior written permission of the publisher. No one shall upload this title(s), or part of this title(s), to any social media websites.

For all enquiries regarding motion picture, television, and other media rights, please contact Samuel French.

MUSIC USE NOTE

Licensees are solely responsible for obtaining formal written permission from copyright owners to use copyrighted music in the performance of this play and are strongly cautioned to do so. If no such permission is obtained by the licensee, then the licensee must use only original music that the licensee owns and controls. Licensees are solely responsible and liable for all music clearances and shall indemnify the copyright owners of the play(s) and their licensing agent, Samuel French, against any costs, expenses, losses and liabilities arising from the use of music by licensees. Please contact the appropriate music licensing authority in your territory for the rights to any incidental music.

IMPORTANT BILLING AND CREDIT REQUIREMENTS

If you have obtained performance rights to this title, please refer to your licensing agreement for important billing and credit requirements.

CONTENTS

A Study of Limits 7

Entropy Increasing in a Closed System 17

Forsooth!. 29

A Study of Limits

Emily Sheera Cutler

CAST OF CHARACTERS

KEVIN – A college senior. He is mature, professional, and grounded, specifically concerned about maintaining his tutoring business.

KELSEY – A high school student. She is young, dreamy, and in love with Kevin.

(A slightly messy college dorm room with stacks of books on the desk and piles of paper laid out on an unmade bed.)

(KEVIN, a senior in college, slowly paces about the room, fiddling with the blinds and trying to straighten up his bed. We hear a soft knock at the door. KEVIN looks out the window one more time before approaching the door. He puts on a close-lipped, friendly smile, reaches his hand out, and confidently opens the door.)

(KELSEY, a high school junior, stands awkwardly in the doorway. Her arms lie tense by her sides, and she bites her lip. She looks down, and KEVIN stares at her, still forcing himself to keep his smile, trying to get over the initial shock of seeing KELSEY.)

KELSEY. Um.

KEVIN. *(coming back to the reality of the situation)* It's so good to see you, Kelsey.

KELSEY. Thanks.

(KEVIN sits down in the chair in front of his desk. KELSEY walks into the room, reaching out to close the door behind her, but only lightly tapping it and not fully closing it. She stands tensely beside KEVIN's desk.)

KELSEY. Your dorm room looks kind of different.

KEVIN. It does?

(beat)

Oh, yeah, I finally got a new carpet. The other one was almost unbearably dirty.

KELSEY. Oh.

(Pause. KELSEY looks around for a place to sit. She turns from facing the desk to standing beside the desk and leans against the wall. She crosses her arms. KEVIN

sits up straight in his chair, fiddling with the cover of a book on his desk.)

KEVIN. So, how are you?

KELSEY. *(timidly)* I told you already. I'm fine.

KEVIN. But really. Can you just tell me how you are? I'm worried. How are your classes?

KELSEY. *(a bit more confident)* Fine. They're just fine. I just love AP Statistics. I really just love it.

KEVIN. That's good.

KELSEY. It's very applicable.

KEVIN. So I've heard.

KELSEY. Much more applicable than calculus. You wouldn't believe it. We're learning so many more applicable things. Stats is very useful.

KEVIN. How have you applied it so far?

KELSEY. Looking at research. Finding whether more people shop at Walmart with credit cards or cash. If online SAT prep works better than a class. If it's more common for males or females to read the *New York Times*. It's all very useful.

(Pause. **KELSEY** *moves a step forward, arms still crossed.* **KEVIN** *gets up from the chair to plug his laptop in.)*

KEVIN. I was just worried because you hadn't called or come by. I was hoping because you're busy with your new classes. I'm sure junior year is very chaotic.

KELSEY. *(tensely)* Yeah, it is. I'm just busy.

KEVIN. I'm sure. Well I needed to make sure you were doing okay. I haven't gotten a chance to see you since classes started, and the way you sounded after I said I wouldn't be able to tutor you in Calculus 2 this year – how your voice sounded – and I hated thinking I was disappointing you – I never followed up. That's why I called. I wanted to check in with you. I didn't want you to think you were bothering me.

KELSEY. I'm fine.

KEVIN. I'm glad to hear it.

(**KELSEY** *looks down, biting her lip.* **KEVIN** *finishes plugging his laptop in and looks at* **KELSEY**.)

KELSEY. *(on a different note, so as to change the subject – more sincere, genuinely concerned)* How are your parents? How's your grandma?

KEVIN. Good, very good. She's getting better. She really likes her aid, Margerie. Margerie comes in to cut her hair and everything, and she seems happy enough in her little room. I think moving her – I mean, I think her moving there was a good decision.

KELSEY. *(looking up, smiling a little)* I'm really glad to hear that she's fine, Kevin.

KEVIN. Thanks for asking. Your concern means a lot.

(*They pause.* **KELSEY** *looks down again.* **KEVIN** *moves to sit on the bed, relaxing a little.* **KELSEY** *moves toward the chair and sits down. She breathes out a little and relaxes her shoulders.*)

KEVIN. I missed you over the summer.

KELSEY. Yeah?

KEVIN. Sometimes I would be going back over my calculus stuff, and I would think of you. Every time I even see an infinity sign I think of that love poem you wrote and smile.

KELSEY. *(looking up at him)* Really?

KEVIN. Yeah.

(*Beat.* **KELSEY** *climbs up on the bed and sits cross-legged beside* **KEVIN**. **KEVIN** *looks off toward the side.*)

KEVIN. Sometimes I think I learned more from tutoring you than you ever learned from me.

(**KELSEY** *laughs.*)

KEVIN. That sounded cheesy, didn't it?

KELSEY. *(blushing)* No, of course not. I mean maybe for a fourth grade math teacher. Not for you though.

KEVIN. *(laughing)* Right, not for me. I'm just a college senior and a calculus tutor.

KELSEY. Yeah. There's something different about calculus, isn't there?

KEVIN. That's right. There's something different about calculus. But I guess stats does have more real-life applications.

(Pause. **KELSEY** *looks away again.)*

KELSEY. I just love AP Statistics.

(beat)

KEVIN. I'm sorry, Kelsey.

KELSEY. *(smiling fakely, so as not to look sad at all)* It's fine. I love stats just as much as calculus.

KEVIN. I'll be busy this year, with my grandma and all. Tutoring you in Calculus 2 would just be too much.

(They look at each other.)

KELSEY. You don't have to defend yourself. I know it's my fault. I couldn't do calculus without you.

KEVIN. I'm not defending myself, Kelsey. I really am busy. It really would be too much.

KELSEY. I know it's my fault.

(beat)

KEVIN. You weren't a burden.

KELSEY. *(broken, softly)* I know I was. I know I was, I mean, I know I was too dependent. That time – I mean, when that – well, I didn't need to come here and tell you that about Marcus. I could've dealt with it myself. I mean, I didn't need to dump all that on you, I guess, well, I shouldn't have –

KEVIN. You needed to tell someone about that, Kelsey. Bullying… well bullying is serious, and you needed to talk about it. But there was really nothing I could do. I felt ill-equipped to help you handle the situation.

KELSEY. You were there, that's all, and I mean, you're just so smart, and you know how to deal with things, I mean, and I guess I thought… well… I mean – I thought – I knew – that you… I really thought that you cared. I thought I could talk to you about anything, I mean, not just about calculus.

KEVIN. Look, I'm glad you felt you could trust me with that.

(beat)

KELSEY. We always talked about other things besides calculus. You told me about your grandmother and the situation with your parents, and about the anxiety you got over having to work while in school. It was never just about calculus.

*(**KEVIN** squirms, crossing his arms and making an attempt to scoot further from **KELSEY** on the bed.)*

KEVIN. You're just different.

KELSEY. I guess I am. I shouldn't have told you, really. I know – I mean, I'm sorry, well, not sorry, but – I just, I know it's my fault, because I wanted you to be more. I wanted –

KEVIN. There's nothing wrong with wanting a friend.

KELSEY. *(flatly)* Oh, yeah. A friend.

(beat)

Friends aren't this dependent on each other.

KEVIN. Being friends is great, but there's always going to be the issue that we talked about the last time we spoke. It's society. Right now my tutoring center is doing pretty well, and I could use it for my resume. But to have a student's parent suggest that we –

KELSEY. *(getting off the bed, standing tensely)* I don't want to talk about misunderstandings.

KEVIN. I want you to know that I don't blame you. It's not your fault that someone got the wrong idea. You shouldn't have to worry about that, but it's the way things are. My tutoring center could have an impact on my career, on my future. But listen, I don't blame <u>you</u>. I'm just saying we need to be careful in case –

KELSEY. I hate AP Statistics. I absolutely hate it with all my heart. I've never hated a class so much. The only thing they ever talk about is the AP test. Don't do this and don't do that because it will look bad on the test, and then you know what will happen, that horrible awful worst horror story ever, a three. It's so easy, and they're sitting there telling us what variables are so we can define them the right way on the test, and you have to know what everything's *called*, everything's name, and nothing even connects. They don't even do anything in AP Statistics. They sit there and *talk*. It's all about following the rules, knowing your place. When to use which test, how to use every formula. No room for thinking outside the lines or coming up with my own ways to solve problems – I don't have to *think*. There's no magical feeling like I got with the polar system. No desire to get someone like you to teach me more about connections.

KEVIN. Wow. I –

KELSEY. You know something? They don't even have the concept of infinity in statistics. I mean, who needs infinity when all you're doing is making some stupid bar graph? I hate that. I hate not having to think. It's all the same, every day, everything. It's not even okay to be different in statistics. You set up every problem the same way, every histogram with the same widths, and it's always listing, listing, listing to find the same median and the same interquartile range. Like you walk into the classroom and there's a rule that says no creativity allowed. Each new thing is just this other step you have to memorize, something I don't even have a connection with. You know what I'd be doing in Calculus 2 right now? Intersecting planes. Learning how to see. Learning perspective, learning about space, about the relationships between the different dimensions. A union of geometry and algebra. A union of two wholly unique ways of thinking that are meant to be together.

KEVIN. *(sadly)* Calculus is both time and timelessness somehow bound together.

(beat)

KEVIN. Kelsey?

*(**KELSEY** sits on the bed again.)*

KELSEY. I'm glad I came tonight.

*(Pause. **KELSEY** rests her head on **KEVIN**'s shoulder.)*

Integrals or derivatives?

KEVIN. *(laughing)* This again?

KELSEY. For old time's sake.

KEVIN. Integrals. Alternating series test or comparison test?

KELSEY. Comparison. L'Hopital or Euler?

KEVIN. Euler. Taylor series or implicit differentiation?

KELSEY. Taylor series. All the way. Polar or Cartesian?

KEVIN. Polar.

(beat)

KELSEY. Me too.

*(**KEVIN** looks at his watch, then back at **KELSEY**.)*

KEVIN. Wow, it's late.

KELSEY. Yeah.

KEVIN. I have a couple assignments I need to get done before tomorrow. I haven't even started yet.

KELSEY. That sucks.

*(**KEVIN** looks at his desk. He starts to get up. **KELSEY** follows him in getting off of the bed. **KEVIN** escorts her to the door. They are both more relaxed than they were in the beginning.)*

KEVIN. It was good seeing you, Kelsey.

KELSEY. Yeah.

KEVIN. *(almost hesitating)* Just give stats a chance. Maybe you can make friends, find others who share your views. You'll find connections in stats, too. It will just take time.

(He opens the door, again showing his close-lipped smile. As **KELSEY** *walks out the door, she turns around and says:)*

KELSEY. But there really is nothing like calculus.

*(***KELSEY*** turns back around and walks out the door. The door slowly closes behind her.* **KEVIN** *sits in his chair.)*

KEVIN. No. Nothing in the world.

End of Play

Entropy Increasing in a Closed System

Justin Krasner-Karpen

CAST OF CHARACTERS

JO
SALLY

(A file closet in some office. Scattered around, easily dominating the place, is a system of file cabinets, or boxes, or nothing, whatever would be most easily set up and struck. These are labeled in alphabetical order using Post-Its or those index cards you slide into metal slots. Those that will be opened contain a multitude of files and physical information. **JO***, female and about 19, is collapsed on the floor, bent to reach up to one of the cabinets.)*

(Hold on. A closet would be unfurnished, and this place, while possibly underfurnished, and clearly not well furnished, is decidedly furnished. There's a bed here, or maybe a desk or chair, or maybe some boxes that function as bed or desk or chair, some or none of which the audience can see. This is a dormitory bedroom. **SALLY***,* **JO***'s friend (also female) and 19 as of today, stands in the hallway outside the door. This is* **JO***'s bedroom.)*

(A door occupying a specific physical location.)

(The hallway outside: the smell of people living on their own for the first time; whiteboards and posters have yet to discover anything save lighthearted vandalism; not quite enough space.)

(On the floor next to **SALLY** *is a birthday cake. The cake has to be small enough to hold in one hand; maybe it's a fancy cupcake.)*

(Both **SALLY** *and* **JO** *are on the floor, notably crumpled.)*

JO. we fucked up

SALLY. i guess so maybe i don't know

JO. we fucked up we were fucked down then we became fucked increasingly then we fucked up

SALLY. man

JO. what happened

SALLY. we were friends at least you were my friend

JO. you were my friend too i think

SALLY. so we were friends

JO. what happened

> i was looking for something yes i was looking for something but it wasn't there and that was weird

SALLY. are we still friends

JO. we can fix this i know we can fix this there's just there's gotta be some sort of mechanism for antifuckification

SALLY. oh i remember you were looking for something

JO. and you were going to knock on my door

(They move now. Maybe there's a light change: one sort of lighting for the crumpled scenes, one for the less crumpled.)

*(***SALLY*** holds the birthday cake in one hand. ***SALLY****'s other hand is outstretched towards the door. ***SALLY*** moves to knock, then pulls back. ***SALLY*** knocks.)*

SALLY. Are you there, Jo? I need you. I brought cake.

JO. AAUUAUUUGHRAAAUAAURGHGHAGHRGHHHHU HHAHRGHHHH!!!

SALLY. It's me, Sally. Sally Sanderson? It's, um. It's my birthday! Today. Today it is my birthday today.

JO. It isn't there!

SALLY. I um, sent you an e-vite. With a little cake on it. Like this one! *(***SALLY*** points.)* Oh you can't see it, but I'm holding a cake. Because it's my birthday. And I pointed to it just then when I said the, cake on the invite. You can file that under C, for clever or for, cake. Ha, ha ha!

(By now **JO** *has risen and is sorting through the opened files.)*

JO. No, no it has to be here. I have everything in my files. No. It's here. Yes. It has to be. No. Yes.

SALLY. The e-vite had a little song that played when you opened it, I'm not sure if it got through to you all right but I hope it did because it was one heck of a song!

JO. It's not! Where is my spoon! My spoon is missing!

SALLY. Jo please open the door I can hear you in there and I know you must be having a sub-fantastic time but. Ha ha! Just please open the door.

JO. This is beyond redonk. This is supradonk.

SALLY. For me?

My e-vite that I sent to, you, and also to um well, also no, one else My e-vite it had that little song it was great you know the um dooooooo do do do dum doooo do do and it was really hard to get the song to play right when you opened the card and saw the cake that was also on the, electronic invitation, but it was, it will be um, it will have been, to-totes worth it?

JO. THIS IS THE OPPOSITE OF TOTES. THIS IS TOTES UNTOTES.

(Pause?)

SALLY. Should I? Yeah, I'll just. I'll see you later. I hope your spoon um shows up. Ha ha! ha. Happy birthday.

(She moves to leave. Pause.)

*(If lights are changing, they go back here, because **SALLY** and **JO** return to a crumpled position. They do not face each other.)*

JO. stop sally that's not what happened

SALLY. no

JO. yeah no

SALLY. no

JO. no yeah yeah no that was absurd

SALLY. so it didn't happen that way? you didn't get your spoon

JO. absurd we went through it and it became absurd reduced to the absurd

SALLY. reductio ad absurdum

JO. so we started with false assumptions like schrödinger's cat

SALLY. man

JO. we assume the copenhagen interpretation of quantum mechanics then if you put a cat into a catmurder device operating at fifty percent efficiency until you take it out the cat is both alive and dead

SALLY. shoulda made up its freaking mind

JO. it's just dumb absurd monsieur copenhagen was an idiot

SALLY. i think when you didn't let me in that was wrong we did that wrong you let me in because i ended up in the room

JO. i must've

(They return to a more expected human position.)

SALLY. Are you there, Jo? I need you. I brought cake. I don't have any spoon to eat with.

JO. I heard. I went to the store to get some, but all they had were those awful plastic spoons. Here, come in.

SALLY. Did you, um. Get my e-vite?

JO. Oh! I liked the song. Doot doo. Doo. Doo doodoo doot do-doo doo,

BOTH. Doot do do-do doo!

SALLY. This is just so great. I mean, you're here, and you're, you. And it's today, it's my birthday. Just, this. I think, this. Is the happiest I could ever be. This is the happiest I could ever be! This is the happiest I could ever be?

JO. The harmonic series.

SALLY. What?

JO. The harmonic series, you take one, add a half, one third, one fourth, and so on. The harmonic series. It diverges. Even though you add a smaller and smaller amount each time, as you keep adding you can go off to infinity.

I took a ceramics course. To get you a spoon, for your birthday? But. Ceramics is hard. All my things ended up really lumpy and bumpy and stumpy and really not at all right for a birthday cake.

SALLY. Should we go somewhere, or.

JO. No. That's not. We don't need to go anywhere.

Anyway you can think of the harmonic series as stacking a series of bricks. You have a brick on top sticking off halfway from the one beneath it, and that one sticking out one third from the one under it, and keep going with more and more bricks sticking out less and slightly less, and you get an protrusion of bricks that doesn't fall over.

SALLY. I wish I could be a cat. Like, I wouldn't need someone else telling me to be happy. I could just be.

JO. I tried metallurgy also. For the spoon.

SALLY. And I would have claws. Retractable claws. Retractable spoon-claws. And if there was something that was there, that I couldn't handle, I could take out my spoons, and I could handle it. I could take out my spoons, and scoop it up, and I could handle it, and if I needed it later, I could just crush it between my spoons, and just squeeze it down with so much pressure, just forever, until the moment became just a single diamond, perfect, unbreakable, floating in space while everything flied around it.

JO. The harmonic series, because it diverges, it goes out forever, to infinity, you can make a stack of bricks one on top of the other, each getting a little farther from the one on the ground, and you could go you could go all the way across this room, or to the cafeteria, or to London, or to the moon, or however far you wanted…

(She cuts herself off.)

(Assuming the world is flat (and has a constant gravitational field (and extends forever (and you had enough bricks.))))

SALLY. Wait. That's just math, you couldn't. Bricks aren't perfect. They'll break apart, especially if you tried to step on them they'd break apart, because of entropy. Oh my god.

JO. I made a time machine. I wasn't sure if I could, but I checked my files, and it was there. Right behind "Tin Cans," "Time Machine Blueprints." I got the parts and I got it and I went back in time. I found a master medieval silversmith, and I became his apprentice. I spent years studying under him, and I changed the etymology of the word "Silver" so it was "Sallyver" and I invented a new atomic model where instead of kind of a circle the atom looks like your face. I spent decades working, and in my dying moments as a master sallyversmithess I finished the spoon. It was a great spoon. And then I died, and I spent a thousand years in the world between worlds and I forgot what I was and why I was there, and then I was born, and then I met you and I remembered.

SALLY. You're not listening! Entropy increases! Everything, absolutely everything, it's a science or a statistics, everything gets messier and messier and messier and as long as time exists nothing will ever get less messy without the messiness becoming some messy mess somewhere else. Nothing stays the same. Cats die! Your files, anything everything in the exact right place, this Aristotlean wet dream it's not real. Even diamonds, they aren't even in the lowest energy state for carbon. You can set a diamond on fire! And instead of this beautiful, perfect thing, of course the universe wouldn't like that, you get graphite, pencil lead, and it does nothing but break apart and slide apart and leave as little layers, smeared and streaked across, a huge, just a huge mess.

JO. The Victoria and Albert Museum is not very kind about lending out parts of its silverware collection.

SALLY. So, you didn't—

JO. I didn't get you anything for your birthday.

Let's go away, let's build a bridge of bricks up to the North Pole and we can get married and have an expected value of oh point eight baby girls and oh point seven baby boys and we can live together forever making spoons and birthday cake and dying in each other's arms. Question mark?

(They recrumple.)

SALLY. wow

JO. wow

SALLY. that didn't solve any of our problems

JO. no it just made things worse

SALLY. did you really feel that way

JO. yes no both did you really feel that way

SALLY. no yes i hope not

JO. and at any rate we didn't find my spoon

SALLY. maybe it wasn't about that maybe it wasn't about spoons

JO. oh of course not

(Uncrumple.)

SALLY. Are you there, Jo? I need you. I brought cake.

JO. Let's eat it without a spoon because that's acceptable human behavior.

(Recrumple.)

SALLY. i'm sorry that was dumb let's just drop it
i mean i meant maybe just it wasn't about anything

JO. god what happened

SALLY. i think

JO. this is terrible

SALLY. i think you weren't on the inside yes i think i was on the inside and you entered

JO. how did i mess this up god this is awful

SALLY. i took it

JO. it was right there

SALLY. i took it i took it i took it

JO. what

(SALLY dumps the cake by JO and moves to the file cabinet. JO remains on the floor.)

SALLY. Okay, okay. Great. Okay. I took it. I took your goddamn spoon, okay? Why? Why? Huh, you're asking why. Okay, I was looking for this week's problem set for Stockings of the 17th Century 103 and I thought, hey, Jo has a file on everything, I bet she'll have that. *(She pulls out a heretofore hidden file.)* Sanderson comma Sally. Female. 5'3". Hair: black. Eyes: black. *(or whatever the actor is)* Friendship status: intimate. There I was, just between "Sabertooth Tiger" and "Sashimi."

I was stuck in your little file cabinet between a dead cat and overpriced raw fish! You get it, okay? Okay? No, not okay! I was just, just, there. F 5 3 black black intimate. *(or whatever)* Nothing else. Why not "C" for "celery-lover" or "D" for "dermatology major" or "K" for "kinds of need a hug right now okay because it's her birthday okay and no one came to her party okay so she stole her best and basically only friend's favorite dedicated birthday cake spoon because how else is anyone even going to know that she was alive!?"

Oh, um. Sorry about that, just.

sorry

(SALLY goes over to JO and SALLY holds out the file in one hand and SALLY holds out the spoon in the other hand. JO does not move. JO has not moved through the preceding speech. SALLY places the file on JO's lap and places the spoon on top. SALLY moves slowly towards the hallway exit. JO turns her head toward SALLY. JO runs to SALLY, taking her by the shoulder.)

(JO holds the file. She releases as heat energy stored by the position of the particles in the file. Ideally she would split it into strips of paper then microscopic flecks

then individual molecules then atoms then protons then individual quarks and the pieces would spread throughout the room and throughout the building and throughout the Earth's atmosphere then throughout the galaxy until the individual particles are spread with equal probability throughout the entire universe, and while this is certain to happen eventually, it may be inconvenient to perform in a time the audience is willing to watch, and therefore **JO** *scatters the file.)*

*(***JO** *holds out the spoon.* **SALLY** *delicately cuts off a bite of the cake. She smooshes it in* **JO**'s *face.)*

(blackout)

(Wait, that wasn't quite right. It's fast, but it's not a blackout, it's a fade. A quick fade to black. Perhaps there's just enough time for the audience to catch a glimpse, or the thought of a glimpse, as **SALLY** *and* **JO** *and spoon and cake and file collapse into a wriggling, giggling mass of* **SALLIE***s and* **JO***s and spoons and bits of cake and scraps of paper.)*

End of Play

Forsooth!

Connor Foley

CHARACTER LIST

LYDIA – Female, age 19. Only child of Sir Harold and romantic lead.

DAVIS – Male, age 19. The evil main villain, who is also a respectable noble.

FABIO – Male, age 19. Ruggedly handsome servant who serves as the hero.

GRETCHEN – Female, age 19. Lydia's humble maid Gretchen.

THE DIRECTOR – Male, age 40. Writer and Director of "Forsooth!", the greatest play ever written.

SIR HAROLD – Male, age 40. Lydia's father, whose estate is without a male heir.

FATHER PETER – Male, age 60. A depressed monk.

LAFAYETTE – Male, age 40. Captain of the guard for Harold's estate.

LADY MORGAN – Female, age 300. Looks more like 30, is not a vampire.

I

(End of the final scene: lights up. The entire cast, with the exception of **LYDIA**, **FABIO**, *and* **DAVIS** *lie dead on the stage, in various overdramatic death poses, dressed in Shakespearian clothing.* **FABIO** *stands in a dramatic pose next to* **LYDIA**, *while* **DAVIS** *hides badly behind an overturned prop.)*

FABIO. Alas, my fair Lydia, that it has come to this. For here lie dead on this field of most unfortunate battle everyone we have ever known. The entire village is destroyed, and now, we must make our own fortunes in the far away lands known as Beverly Hills. If only my father were here to see this!

LYDIA. Yes, dear Fabio, but you killed him not five minutes ago.

FABIO. Alas! 'Tis true! 'Tis a sad day, and to think that the one responsible remains as of yet at large.

*(***DAVIS** *cackles evilly.)*

FABIO. Forsooth! What doth this cackling portray?

*(***DAVIS** *jumps out from behind the barrel, holding a very small dagger.)*

DAVIS. This shall be the end of you, valiant hero! En Guard!

*(***FABIO** *stabs* **DAVIS**, *who dies overdramatically.)*

FABIO. Alas! The day is won!

LYDIA. 'Tis true! Thou hath saved the day, Fabio. Forsooth!

(They embrace, and the lights go down. Everyone gets up and walks off the stage, and the props are reorganized. **LYDIA** *is suddenly acting less Shakespearian.)*

LYDIA. Hang on, why'd everything go all dark? Fabio? Where did you go?

(Lights up on "scene one.")

LYDIA. What the hell was that?!?

*(**SIR HAROLD** enters.)*

HAROLD. Good morrow, my fair daughter! And speaking of fairs, I do hope you're ready for the big festival tomorrow.

LYDIA. Jesus Christ! Dad! You're alive!

HAROLD. Yes.

LYDIA. But didn't Davis poison you?

HAROLD. You mean Davis the royal vassal? Forsooth! Of course not!

LYDIA. But… But… Wasn't the fair last week?

HAROLD. It seems like every day is a fair when you live in such a fine estate as this, doesn't it?

LYDIA. Well… No, not really.

HAROLD. Forsooth! You speak foolishly. And that does seem to be a little… *Out of character*, now, doesn't it?

*(**HAROLD** stares at **LYDIA** intently for a few seconds, then goes back to normal.)*

HAROLD. Alas, I must go. There are preparations to be made! I shall call Gretchen, who is your maid, and she will help you to get ready for tonight's festivities.

LYDIA. I know who Gretchen is, dad. Don't you think this whole situation is a little familiar?

HAROLD. Forsooth! I must be off. Thou hath thyself a good day, fairest daughter!

*(**HAROLD** exits, and **GRETCHEN** enters.)*

GRETCHEN. Good morrow, mistress! It is I, your maid, Gretchen!

LYDIA. I know that, Gretchen. Why does everyone keep telling me that?

GRETCHEN. Forsooth! It is not my place to guess. How may I assist you?

LYDIA. I think I'm supposed to ask about Fabio about now. Why do I think that!?

GRETCHEN. Ah! Most handsome Fabio! 'Tis a pity he is a mere servant, for otherwise, he would be the perfect husband! So strong and skilled is he! I know that thou hath admired him for such a long time.

LYDIA. Yeah, yeah, that's nice and all, Gretchen, but I'm having a bit of an existential crisis here. Why am I all the way back on Tuesday? And why is everyone alive again? And why do I know what I'm supposed to say!?!

GRETCHEN. Forsooth! I believe thou hath had a nightmare, mistress. Although, that does seem a little… *Out of character* for you, now doesn't it?

*(**GRETCHEN** stares intently at **LYDIA** for a few seconds, then goes back to normal.)*

GRETCHEN. Anyway, I'm just your humble maid, Gretchen, who has served you for years, despite your estate's lack of an inheriting heir. If only you would agree to marry! Then we would have an heir to inherit the estate once your father passes away.

LYDIA. Uh… Why are you giving me backstory?

GRETCHEN. I would not know, for I am merely your maid, Gret –

LYDIA. I know! You're Gretchen, you're my maid, I get it already! Stop saying that!

GRETCHEN. Forsooth! I –

LYDIA. And stop saying Forsooth! Why does everyone keep saying that? What does that word even mean!?

GRETCHEN. I would tell you if I knew, but I'm only –

LYDIA. STOP IT! I can see why you need to keep introducing yourself. You're such a dull character that – OH MY GOD.

*(**LYDIA** stands up, knocking over her chair.)*

GRETCHEN. What is it, mistress?

LYDIA. Gretchen, I think... I think we're in a play.

GRETCHEN. Surely not!

LYDIA. Yes! And... Oh no!

(**LYDIA** *clutches her heart like she's going to have a heart attack.*)

LYDIA. This is a terrible play! Who the hell wrote this piece of crap?

GRETCHEN. How can you tell, mistress? It just started.

LYDIA. See? How do you know that!?

GRETCHEN. Well, the lights just came on.

LYDIA. See? The lights! That's unusual, right? If this weren't a play, would there be lights? We're probably being watched by an audience RIGHT NOW.

(**LYDIA** *starts running around, yelling at the four "walls" of the room.*)

LYDIA. Which one of these is the fourth wall? I know you're watching, perverts! Show's over! Go home!

GRETCHEN. Lydia, you should really stop acting... *Out of character.*

("the stare")

GRETCHEN. Otherwise, bad things will happen.

LYDIA. Wait, you're saying I have to keep acting?

GRETCHEN. No! Don't even act. Just carry on like everything is normal.

LYDIA. But Gretchen, none of this is real! This is like the matrix! I can see the freaking code, Neo, and it's a badly written script! How do I know what the matrix is!?

(**GRETCHEN** *suddenly freezes. There's the sound of thunder, the lights flash on and off, and a booming voice echoes throughout the theater.*)

DIRECTOR. Silence!

LYDIA. Who's that? What's going on?

DIRECTOR. I am God to you! You can call me… The director!

LYDIA. Surely not! That's impossible!

DIRECTOR. Weren't you just saying you were in a play?

LYDIA. I… I… Well, yes, but…

*(The **DIRECTOR** walks onto the stage. **LYDIA** screams and flattens herself on the ground.)*

DIRECTOR. What are you doing?

LYDIA. I'm, uh, bowing, Mr. Director.

DIRECTOR. Well, get up.

*(**LYDIA** stands up, but avoids looking at the **DIRECTOR**, shielding her eyes.)*

DIRECTOR. Now what are you doing?

LYDIA. I'm averting my eyes, Mr. Director.

DIRECTOR. Well stop that too! Alright, I can see you're a little confused, so here's how things are going. You're being played by an understudy tonight. The usual actress got hit by a semi truck.

LYDIA. Oh my god! Is she alright?

DIRECTOR. No, she's quite dead. As I was saying, you might be new, but that doesn't mean I'm letting you do whatever you want. Stay in character, keep the play moving, and above all else, don't break the fourth wall. If that happens, you're outta here. Got it?

LYDIA. Uh…

DIRECTOR. Good. And stop complaining about the writing. I wrote the play myself, and it's the best play that's ever been written. Showtime!

*(The **DIRECTOR** leaves the stage, and there's more thunder and lightning. **GRETCHEN** unfreezes.)*

GRETCHEN. Anyway, have a wonderful afternoon, mistress!

*(**GRETCHEN** exits.)*

LYDIA. This is gonna be a long week…

(lights down)

II

(Lights up on the dining hall. SIR HAROLD stands at the head of the table, talking to various characters. DAVIS, FABIO, and GRETCHEN are also in the room. LYDIA enters.)

HAROLD. Forsooth! Here comes my daughter now! Let us eat and be merry, my guests, for today marks the beginning of the summer festival! Daughter, have thee any fine words of greeting for our guests this evening?

LYDIA. Uh… I… Forsooth?

HAROLD. Wise words indeed, Lydia! Let the festival begin!

(The guests all start having silent background conversations, and DAVIS approaches LYDIA.)

DAVIS. Good evening, dear Lydia. May I say that you are looking particularly beautiful this morning?

(DAVIS cackles evilly.)

LYDIA. Thank you, that's a very kind thing to say… I think.

DAVIS. Well, I only have the kindest of intentions for you and your family, especially as your estate currently has no heir, and I am a respectable noble.

(DAVIS cackles evilly.)

LYDIA. Okay, never mind. This conversation has suddenly taken a turn for the creepy.

DAVIS. Have I mentioned how single I am?

LYDIA. That was actually pretty obvious.

(DAVIS suddenly turns away from LYDIA and begins to monologue.)

DAVIS. Little does she realize that I plan to marry her, and inherit the estate with all its riches! My plan is unstoppable!

(**DAVIS** *cackles evilly.*)

LYDIA. You realize that I'm standing right here, right?

DAVIS. Of course! You are a diamond amongst a sea of women, fair Lydia.

LYDIA. I'm going to pretend I didn't hear that. Anyway, why were you revealing an evil plan a minute ago?

DAVIS. Forsooth! I have not a clue what you are talking about.

(**DAVIS** *cackles evilly.*)

LYDIA. Besides, that's really not that evil a plan.

DAVIS. I beg your pardon? That is the most evil plan I have ever devised!

LYDIA. That seems like a pretty legitimate tactic, actually. Of course, I would never marry you, but you're bound to find someone else who's rich somewhere around here.

DAVIS. So… It's a good plan?

LYDIA. Yes, but your monologue skills need improvement. If you're going to monologue, you're going to need to do an internal monologue. Otherwise it's just plain stupid. Here. Watch.

(**LYDIA** *turns away dramatically. The lights all dim, except for a single spotlight on* **LYDIA**. *Everyone else on stage freezes.*)

LYDIA. So, Davis plans to steal my father's estate. 'Tis a plan doomed to failure, to be sure, but nevertheless, I must be watchful. With my own eye on Fabio, I simply cannot let this happen, lest true love be parted. For though one may follow their own dreams and wishes, they shall surely be struck down in their desires by others chasing their own rainbows with a greater ferocity. Thus, I must be as fierce as a tiger in my holdings, as that no other shall come between us. I only pray that fate favors my tenacity.

(The lights go back to normal, and everyone on stage applauds, before going back to doing nothing important.)

DAVIS. Wow! That was amazing! I've never seen anyone monologue that well!

LYDIA. Thanks. You can probably do that too, if you practice. Oh, and stop cackling evilly. It doesn't help.

DAVIS. Of course! That actually seems pretty obvious now. Thanks for the tips, Lydia.

LYDIA. Anytime. Now, though, I need to go talk to Fabio. True love and all that stuff. Later!

DAVIS. Wait!

LYDIA. Yeah?

DAVIS. Uh… *(awkward pause)* … Forsooth.

LYDIA. Sure. Forsooth to you too. Whatever.

*(**LYDIA** crosses the stage to where **FABIO** and **GRETCHEN** are talking.)*

DAVIS. Wow… She's amazing!

*(**DAVIS** exits.)*

LYDIA. Hey Fabio. 'Sup, Gretchen?

GRETCHEN. Forsooth, my lady! I am your humble maid Gretchen! This is Fabio, who has worked here as a servant for years!

LYDIA. Gretchen, please. Is it too much to ask that you stop introducing yourself every time I see you?

GRETCHEN. Forsooth! I –

LYDIA. Forget it. Just go do maid things or whatever.

GRETCHEN. But… My lady! I'm supposed to –

LYDIA. I really don't care that much, Gretchen.

GRETCHEN. Forsooth! I am off.

LYDIA. And stop saying forsooth! It's going to make me kill someone!

FABIO. Forsooth!

LYDIA. Oh great. Not you too.

FABIO. I apologize, fair Lydia. It is good to see you again! Oh, how thine eyes sparkle like the scales of a dead fish!

LYDIA. Uh… Thanks, Fabio.

FABIO. I aim only to please you, dear Lydia.

LYDIA. Yeah… Well, how about we stick with less descriptive compliments?

FABIO. Forsooth! You speak foolishness. We all know how much you adore elaborate praise.

LYDIA. No, I really don't. Besides, everyone here seems to suck at it.

FABIO. It's a good thing I am the exception to this rule! Forsooth! Your lips, they are as red as if you had just drunk a gallon of fresh blood! Your hair, it is of the same golden color as freshly cut straw for the horse stalls! Your skin –

LYDIA. Stop it!

FABIO. You don't enjoy my compliments?

LYDIA. No, I don't! How is calling me a vampire romantic!?

FABIO. What are you talking about? Vampires are totally romantic!

LYDIA. This can't be happening. This is a nightmare!

HAROLD. *(cutting in)* Lydia, I can't help but notice that you seem to be acting a little… *Out of character.*

*(Everyone in the room but **FABIO** gives **LYDIA** "the stare.")*

LYDIA. Uh… Forsooth?

(Everyone goes back to normal.)

FABIO. How about we go for a little romantic stroll in the gardens at midnight tonight?

LYDIA. *(unenthusiastically)* Sure. That would be "great." Forsooth.

FABIO. Excellent! I shall see you then, sweet Lydia!

(**FABIO** *exits.*)

LYDIA. Oh my god. Fabio's an idiot. I swear, this situation can't possibly get any worse.

(**SIR HAROLD** *steps forward and raises a cup.*)

HAROLD. A toast! To our peaceful and prosperous city! May we all live long and happy lives!

(**HAROLD** *drinks from the cup, then drops it on the floor, gasping.*)

HAROLD. Forsooth! Poison! Alas! Forsooth! I am poisoned! Forsooth!

(**HAROLD** *dies overdramatically.*)

LYDIA. ...Shit.

(*lights down*)

III

*(Lights up on the graveyard at **HAROLD**'s funeral. **FATHER PETER** stands by the casket, delivering a prayer in his constantly gloomy tone.)*

PETER. …And though he hath died, he shalt be remembered by all as the man he truly was, not the corpse you doth see before you. For though his flesh rots, and his bones turn to dust, and he is to eventually be completely forgotten, he shalt live on in our hearts as the man who died without an heir to inherit his estate. Until we, too, die. Forsooth.

EVERYONE. Forsooth.

*(Everyone exits except **LYDIA** and **FATHER PETER**.)*

LYDIA. Thanks, Father Peter. I'm sure dad would have loved that ceremony.

PETER. Don't mention it, Lydia. I'll be sure to hold a similar ceremony for you when you die.

LYDIA. Oh. Uh… Thanks?

PETER. Of course, when I die, nobody's going to give me a proper funeral. I doubt they'll even notice I'm gone until they want me to bury someone else. Forsooth.

LYDIA. Okay… I'm going to go mourn my father or something. Have a nice day!

PETER. Don't get your hopes up. I never have nice days.

*(**PETER** gloomily exits, leaving **LYDIA** beside the casket. **DAVIS** enters.)*

DAVIS. Hello, Lydia! You're looking nice this afternoon!

LYDIA. Oh, hi, Davis. No offense, but can you please get lost?

DAVIS. Uh… Forsooth, but could you tell me why?

LYDIA. Look, I know you were just doing your job, but you still killed my dad. So could you leave me alone for a while?

DAVIS. No I didn't!

LYDIA. Of course you did! You're the villain! It's obvious it was you.

DAVIS. Well, actually… uh…

LYDIA. What is it?

DAVIS. Please, don't ask. It's embarrassing.

LYDIA. Just tell me already!

DAVIS. Fine! I was supposed to poison him, but I sort of… uh… forgot to.

LYDIA. Real convincing, Davis. Your performance deserves rave reviews.

DAVIS. I'm serious! I left the stage a little too early after you gave me those lessons on how to monologue. I've been practicing, by the way! Here, watch.

(**DAVIS** *turns away dramatically, and the lights dim, with a spotlight on him.*)

DAVIS. Alas! She doesn't believe me. Though I admit the dastardly deed had indeed been delicately determined in my deceitful dome, my meanings may not have had hardly a hazard to them. Forsooth! 'Tis folly to be trapped within one's own perceptions! I must devise a means through with which to convince Lydia of my innocence! But how?

(*lights go back to normal*)

DAVIS. See? It's not perfect yet, but I'm getting better at it.

LYDIA. Yeah, I guess you are.

(*pause*)

LYDIA. Okay, let's pretend that I believe you for a second. If you didn't murder my father, then who did?

DAVIS. How should I know? There were a lot of people in that room. Any one of them could have killed him!

LYDIA. I think I might know.

DAVIS. Really? Who?

LYDIA. Just give me a second, and I'll get back to you on that.

*(**LYDIA** looks up and starts shouting.)*

LYDIA. Hey! Director!

DAVIS. Lydia! Shh! That's a bad idea!

LYDIA. Shut up, I know what I'm doing. Almost. Hey! Look at me! I'm in a play!

DAVIS. Lydia! Stop! I totally killed your father, okay? Yup, it was me. Mystery solved.

LYDIA. Not buying it. Hey! Mr. Director! What's my motivation?

*(There's a rumble of thunder, the lights flash, and the **DIRECTOR** walks on stage holding a script.)*

DIRECTOR. You wanted to talk? Here I am. This had better be good.

LYDIA. If Davis didn't kill my father, then why does he still die?

DIRECTOR. I hadn't given that part much thought, actually.

LYDIA. WHAT!? How can you just randomly kill off a character for no reason?

DIRECTOR. Hey, I'll have you know that I'm improvising this just as much as you are right now. I had a perfectly crafted plot until you went ahead and started messing with everything!

LYDIA. Perfectly crafted? You can't call this mess perfectly crafted!

DIRECTOR. Insulting me won't get you into my good books, Lyd.

LYDIA. I'm just saying, things seem a little disorganized here!

DIRECTOR. Look, I'll admit that I may have been a little hasty in killing off Sir Harold, but I've already got things figured out.

LYDIA. And... ?

DIRECTOR. And I'm not going to tell you! That would ruin the suspense. I'll give you a clue, though. It was either the captain of the guard Lafayette, the widow Lady Morgan, your neighbor Sir Patrick, or one of the other minor characters I've already introduced. Happy?

LYDIA. Not really.

DIRECTOR. Too bad. And stop messing with my play, or I might just have to cut you out of the script.

LYDIA. You wouldn't do that! I'm the main character! Even you wouldn't be stupid enough to make a romantic tragedy without the hero's romantic interest in it!

DIRECTOR. Oh wouldn't I? ...Actually, that came out wrong. No, I wouldn't be that stupid, but I could always make someone else the lead role. Like, say... Gertrude!

LYDIA. Who's that again?

DIRECTOR. Your maid.

LYDIA. I knew that! I was just... uh... testing you.

DIRECTOR. Gotcha! Her name's actually Gretchen. See why I keep introducing her?

LYDIA. It's not my fault! She's just so... so... bland! You can't make her the main character!

DIRECTOR. I can do whatever I want! It's my play! You've been warned. No more meddling, or it's curtains for you! Action!

(The **DIRECTOR** *exits as there's another rumble of thunder and the lights flash.)*

DAVIS. Did you really have to do that?

LYDIA. Hey, at least it got us somewhere.

DAVIS. Well? What did he say?

LYDIA. It was either Captain Lafayette, Lady Morgan, Sir Patrick, or Father Peter.

DAVIS. *(sarcastic)* Well, *that* sure narrows it down. We should have this whole thing figured out before the end of the scene!

LYDIA. You're not helping.

DAVIS. Sorry. What can I do?

LYDIA. Thanks for the offer, Davis, but isn't it a little… *out of character* for you?

(**LYDIA** *gives* **DAVIS** *"the stare."*)

DAVIS. Uh… Forsooth!

(**DAVIS** *cackles evilly.* **LYDIA** *stops staring and acts overdramatic.*)

LYDIA. Begone! I shalt not allow thy presence here!

DAVIS. Thou hast not seen the last of me! Forsooth!… Bye Lydia!

(**DAVIS** *exits, and* **LYDIA** *is smiling as lights dim.*)

IV

(Lights up on the flower garden. **DAVIS** *hides behind bushes on stage.* **FABIO** *is pacing back and forth, waiting for* **LYDIA**.*)*

FABIO. Forsooth, 'tis a grand evening indeed. The sky is as clear as fair Lydia's complexion! I only hope that she hath not forgotten our plans for a midnight stroll. Oh, how my heart aches for her sweet voice, which sounds as though she is drowning in honey! But forsooth! I doth harken an approach! I shalt hide in the bushes, and see if it doth be mine hearts desire!

*(***FABIO*** hides badly behind some bushes, as* **GRETCHEN** *enters.)*

GRETCHEN. Fabio! Good Fabio! Where hast thou gotten to? It is I, Gretchen! Lady Lydia's humble maid!

*(***FABIO*** jumps out of the bushes.* **GRETCHEN** *screams.)*

GRETCHEN. Forsooth! A bandit!

FABIO. Nay! 'Tis simply I, Fabio. What news hast thou arrived to bring me?

GRETCHEN. Oh, Fabio! Surely I should have recognized you by thy strong figure!

FABIO. Indeed, I do cut quite the heroic image. But what news of fair Lydia?

GRETCHEN. She hath sent me to tell you that she is still grieving from her father's death, and cannot bring herself to stroll through the garden where she strolled which still he lived. However, I shall accompany you on your walk if you should like, noble Fabio.

FABIO. Nay! This shalt not do! Forsooth! Fair Lydia must join me, for I cannot be without her! Go back, and have her come to me.

GRETCHEN. Art thou certain, noble Fabio? She is quite distraught, and I make very pleasant company on an evening's walk.

FABIO. Forsooth! Leave me now, and do not return without Lydia at your side!

GRETCHEN. As thou doth wish, Fabio. Forsooth!

*(***GRETCHEN*** exits.)*

FABIO. Oh, how I pray that Lydia decides to join me! Without her, I am but a – Forsooth, that was fast. I doth harken another approach. But let me be sure it is indeed Lydia this time.

*(***FABIO*** hides in the bushes again and ***LYDIA*** enters with* **GRETCHEN**.*)*

GRETCHEN. He was here but a moment ago, Lady Lydia. I am certain of it!

LYDIA. Well, he's not here now. Does this mean that I get to go home?

*(***FABIO*** jumps out of the bushes.)*

FABIO. Not a chance!

*(***LYDIA*** screams and punches him, but* **FABIO** *seems unaffected.)*

LYDIA. Ow! My hand!

FABIO. Ha ha! Lady Lydia, thy jesting is most endearing.

LYDIA. Fabio? You son of a bitch! What the hell was that?

FABIO. Yes! It is I. I merely wanted to assure myself that it was you before revealing my presence.

LYDIA. Why!?

FABIO. Forsooth! It is not important. What's important is that we are both here, and that I am complete once again!

LYDIA. Whatever. Just don't jump out at people anymore. It's not romantic in the least. Gretchen, you may go.

GRETCHEN. But Mistress, thou art still grieving!

LYDIA. I said leave us alone, Gretchen.

GRETCHEN. Forsooth. So I shall, my lady.

(**GRETCHEN** *exits.*)

FABIO. Now then, let us walk and wonder at the stars tonight! For surely the beauty of flowers is enhanced tenfold by the moonlight, and thou art no exception!

LYDIA. Thanks. Fabio, but I still can't feel my hand from when I punched you. Can you go get me an ice pack or something?

FABIO. My lady is in need of aid? Forsooth! Say no more! I am off like the wind riding lightning! Fear not, for I shalt return in a like manner – with haste!

(**FABIO** *exits. As* **LYDIA** *stands around waiting,* **DAVIS** *jumps out from behind the same bush that* **FABIO** *was using.*)

DAVIS. Hello, Lydia!

LYDIA. Davis!? What are you doing out here?

DAVIS. I was spying on Fabio. I saw him sneak off, and I wondered where he was going.

LYDIA. So you started spying?

DAVIS. Sorry, it's one of the things I'm best at. I don't think that Fabio even saw me. Although, it is Fabio we're talking about, so that's not saying much.

LYDIA. Good point. He's not the brightest tack in the drawer, is he?

DAVIS. More like he's stupid.

LYDIA. That's probably a little closer to the mark. But was spying on him really necessary?

DAVIS. Well, I've actually had a new theory.

LYDIA. About what?

DAVIS. I think that Fabio may have been the one to kill your father!

LYDIA. Wow.

DAVIS. I know! You never saw it coming, right?

LYDIA. No, I mean wow, I can't believe you would think that. The director said that it was a *minor* character, remember? Fabio is anything but minor.

DAVIS. Maybe the director was trying to throw you off his trail!

LYDIA. No, I really don't think so. Besides, why do you keep trying to help me with this? You're supposed to be scheming or something, aren't you?

DAVIS. I don't know what you're talking about.

LYDIA. Of course you do! You're the bad guy, Davis. You're supposed to be doing evil things!

DAVIS. Well, that doesn't mean we can't be friends, does it?

LYDIA. Of course it does! That's the very definition of being the bad guy!

DAVIS. But –

LYDIA. Just get out of here. Fabio's going to be back any minute now, and I can't have you messing things up.

DAVIS. But you don't even like Fabio! What does it matter if I mess things up?

LYDIA. Fabio's the hero, Davis. In the end, it's going to be me and him, riding off into the sunset with a jolly "Forsooth!" to see us off. That's just how this kind of play ends.

DAVIS. That doesn't seem very fair to you.

LYDIA. Just go away! Go be evil, and do it somewhere else!

DAVIS. If that's what you really want, Lydia. Forsooth.

*(**DAVIS** exits with a lackluster evil cackle. **LYDIA** waits a few seconds, then looks back to where **DAVIS** exited.)*

LYDIA. Davis?

*(**FABIO** enters from the other side.)*

FABIO. Forsooth!

LYDIA. Oh, there you are, Fabio.

FABIO. Indeed! And I brought refreshing ice-cold beverages!

LYDIA. I asked for an ice pack, Fabio.

FABIO. Forsooth! You are right! I'll be right back!

LYDIA. No, Fabio, it's okay. Let us enjoy our walk under these stars, for surely there art none brighter than the one which shines in thine eyes as thou lookest at me. Forsooth.

FABIO. Forsooth, the star you see there is only a reflection of your own beauty. Follow me then, Lydia, fairest of maidens!

*(**FABIO** exits, and **LYDIA** follows slowly, looking back over her shoulder at where **DAVIS** exited.)*

(lights down)

V

(Lights up. **LYDIA** *and* **FABIO** *stroll onto the stage.)*

FABIO. Here we are, my sweet yet healthy fruitcake! We hath arrived at thy humble abode at last. Forsooth, and may we meet again on the morrow!

LYDIA. Of course we will Fabio.

FABIO. 'Tis true! Our burning love, like that of an arsonist's house fire, shall not be extinguished until it's too late, and the entire city is dead! Forsooth!

LYDIA. Wait, was that… Foreshadowing?

FABIO. I don't know what that word means.

LYDIA. You know, it's where you drop a hint about what happens later in the play.

FABIO. Oh. But we're not in a play.

LYDIA. What? No meaningful stare? You're saying that you actually don't know?

FABIO. Don't know what?

LYDIA. That we're in a play!

FABIO. We're in a play!?

LYDIA. Yup. Things make a little more sense now?

FABIO. Why would they?

LYDIA. Because we're in a play.

FABIO. We're in a play!?

LYDIA. Of course we are! Stuff like this only happens in plays.

FABIO. Forsooth! Speak not such thoughts, lady Lydia! For our love is true, and no imagining on thy part. I shall love thee until the day we die, and the town lies in ruins!

LYDIA. See? You did it again!

FABIO. Did what again?

LYDIA. Foreshadowing!

FABIO. Ah, I know what that word means now! Forsooth! Too bad we're not in a play, or I could use it in context.

LYDIA. Fabio! How many times do I have to tell you!?

FABIO. Tell me what?

LYDIA. That we're in a play!

FABIO. We're in a play!?

LYDIA. You know what? Forget it. You can foreshadow outside of plays too, anyway.

FABIO. You can? That's great news! Here, let me try.

(**FABIO** *clears his throat.*)

FABIO. *(with bad acting)* Hello Lydia! My, you're looking awfully unmarried today! I wonder if that will change anytime soon?

LYDIA. Uh… Sure, Fabio. Whatever.

FABIO. Forsooth! I am keeping thou awake. I depart, my endearing dictionary! I shalt see thee around!

(**FABIO** *exits.*)

LYDIA. Fabio! Where are you going? Come back! We live on the same estate!

(**LYDIA** *sighs and begins to walk off stage, but pauses as* **CAPTAIN LAFAYETTE** *enters, on patrol.* **LYDIA** *enters monologue mode.*)

LYDIA. Aha! It's Lafayette! The Director mentioned that he might have been in on my father's murder. I must tread cautiously, though the good captain has been like an uncle to me all my life. It would pain my heart were he the knave, but I would put no plot twist past the Director. Forsooth! 'Tis a sad day when one is at odds with their own family, for a house whose supports turn inward against each other shalt surely collapse inward. Nevertheless, I must do all I can to avenge my father, even should one so kind to me as Lafayette be the perpetrator. May whatever gods there be forgive me for my suspicions, and have mercy on my soul for what I must do.

(LYDIA walks up to LAFAYETTE.)

LYDIA. Hey Uncle Laffy!

(LAFAYETTE stops patrolling.)

LAFAYETTE. Forsooth! If it isn't young Lydia. What is it that brings thee to my route on such a cold, dark night?

LYDIA. Nothing much. I was just walking around and thinking about the feast we held yesterday. What did you think about it?

LAFAYETTE. It was very enjoyable! The food was delicious, and I got to dance with Lady Morgan. I think she has her eye on me! A wonderful night.

LYDIA. Except for the part where my father died, right?

LAFAYETTE. Actually, I enjoyed that part too. It was pretty funny, the way he died.

(LAFAYETTE does an impersonation of Sir Howard.)

LAFAYETTE. Ooh, look at me! I am poisoned! Forsooth! Forsooth! I am dead!

LYDIA. Uncle Laffy! That's terrible! Why are you so happy about all this!?

LAFAYETTE. Well, it's because I was finally proven right.

LYDIA. About what?

LAFAYETTE. Shh! Not so loud. You see, they are watching us. They are *always* watching us. They killed Sir Howard, and now they're after me as well! But I'm too smart for them! I've built up immunities to arsenic, hemlock, wolfs bane, nightshade, cyanide, snake venom, hanging, drowning, and poison!

LYDIA. Uh… What?

LAFAYETTE. I have been ready for this for years! I have always known they were watching, waiting for their chance, but they will never get me! Forsooth!

LYDIA. Uncle, are you feeling alright?

LAFAYETTE. Of course! I am feeling better then ever! However, I must admit that I do feel guilty about your father's death. It was my job to protect him, but they struck before I was ready.

LYDIA. You mean you didn't poison my father?

LAFAYETTE. Of course I did! Repeatedly, too. I had to help him build up his immunities as well. It's my job to keep your family safe, you know. I had made him resistant against everything except generic poison by the time he died. Come to think of it, that probably should have been my priority. You can find that stuff anywhere.

LYDIA. Well, it's good to know you cared about my father... I guess.

LAFAYETTE. Oh, I care about more then just your father. I care about you just as much!

LYDIA. Wait a second, are you saying you've been poisoning me!? What the hell, uncle!?

LAFAYETTE. You know how we have tea together every Wednesday and Sunday?

LYDIA. We've been doing that since I was two! What is *wrong* with you!?

LAFAYETTE. Don't worry, I had Father Peter help me with the dosage. Monks are experts at making poison.

LYDIA. That doesn't make sense.

LAFAYETTE. Sure it does. If we were in a play, *which we're not...*

*(**LAFAYETTE** gives **LYDIA** "the stare.")*

LAFAYETTE. ...then you would know that it's always the monks who give out any potions. Besides, have you *met* the guy? Forsooth!

LYDIA. Hmm... You have a good point... Anyway, I guess it's sort of thoughtful of you to try so hard to keep me safe. Thanks, Uncle Laffy. You've given me lots to think about.

LAFAYETTE. Are we still on for tea tomorrow?

LYDIA. Are you going to poison me again?

LAFAYETTE. No. Maybe. Yes.

LYDIA. At least you're honest. Okay, I'll keep having tea with you.

LAFAYETTE. Then I will see you tomorrow! My shift is over, and I am off to bed. Don't get murdered by that man who has been hiding in the bushes for the last three hours!

(The two of them laugh.)

LAFAYETTE. Forsooth, Lydia!

LYDIA. Forsooth, Uncle Laffy!

*(**LAFAYETTE** exits. **LYDIA** walks towards the other exit, then stops and turns around.)*

LYDIA. Hang on, what was that part about a man in the bushes?

*(**DAVIS** jumps out of a bush behind **LYDIA** and cackles evilly. **LYDIA** screams and punches him in the face. **DAVIS** falls down clutching his nose.)*

LYDIA. Davis!?

DAVIS. MY NOSE!

LYDIA. What the hell!?

DAVIS. I CAN'T FEEL IT BECAUSE IT HURTS TOO MUCH!

LYDIA. Why do people keep doing that!?

DAVIS. OH GOD I THINK I'M DYING!

LYDIA. You were in my bushes! WHY!?

DAVIS. THIS REALLY SHOULDN'T HURT SO BADLY!

LYDIA. How could that have seemed like a good idea!?

DAVIS. WHAT IS YOUR FIST MADE OF!?

LYDIA. Stop crying you big baby! It's not even bleeding.

DAVIS. That's because we can't afford special effects on our budget!

LYDIA. I thought I told you we couldn't be friends anymore.

DAVIS. You did. That's why I'm here to kidnap you.

LYDIA. How's that working out for you?

> (**GRETCHEN** *steps out from behind a prop, or enters the stage if it can be done in a fittingly 'from out of nowhere' style.*)

GRETCHEN. Forsooth!

> (**LYDIA** *screams again and tries to punch* **GRETCHEN** *in the face, but* **GRETCHEN** *catches her fist and puts her in a headlock.*)

LYDIA. Gretchen!?

GRETCHEN. Forsooth! I am sorry, my lady. Reflexes.

LYDIA. Let go of me! When did you even get here!?

> (**GRETCHEN** *lets* **LYDIA** *go.*)

GRETCHEN. Don't worry Lydia, run away! I'll let him kidnap me so that you can escape, for I am merely your humble maid, Gretchen!

LYDIA. Are you kidding me? Look at him! I don't think he's capable of kidnapping anyone at the moment.

GRETCHEN. Forsooth! It's a ruse!

LYDIA. No, I really don't think so.

DAVIS. It burns!

GRETCHEN. I'll save you!

> (**GRETCHEN** *grabs* **DAVIS**, *trying to drag him across the floor to the exit.*)

GRETCHEN. Forsooth! He's got me! Save yourself!

LYDIA. Stop it!

> (**GRETCHEN** *lets go of* **DAVIS**.)

GRETCHEN. What's wrong, mistress?

LYDIA. You're not supposed to be in this scene. Please, just get out. Besides, you're not important enough of a character to get kidnapped. That's usually reserved for the main character.

DAVIS. Exactly!

LYDIA. *You* can shut up, thank you very much! Gretchen, leave!

GRETCHEN. *(resentfully)* Forsooth. I am gone, mistress.

*(***GRETCHEN*** exits. There's an awkward pause.)*

DAVIS. So, how did your date with pretty-boy go?

LYDIA. It went fine. Mostly. We talked. A lot. I don't know. It's just… He doesn't seem *real*. He's sweet enough, but that's about all he has going for him. I just can't make myself love him.

DAVIS. Then don't.

LYDIA. You don't get a vote on this, Davis! What I do is *my* business.

DAVIS. You mean the director's business, right? He's calling all the shots. Whatever happened to person who taught me to monologue? You were perfectly willing to break a few rules then.

LYDIA. Who says I'm not still willing? Maybe I just *want* to be with Fabio. Just stay out of my life!

*(***LYDIA*** exits. Lights down on ***DAVIS***, alone in the middle of the stage.)*

VI

(Lights up. **LYDIA** *is sleeping in her bed on the left side of the stage.* **FABIO** *enters from the other side, carrying a tray of breakfast. He sets it down on the desk beside the bed, and starts to speak.)*

FABIO. Forsooth! Such a fair sight she is, lost in that eternal wooded refuge we call sleep! Surely, t'would be a shame to ruin such a perfect scene of beauty! Not even the delicious smell of a home cooked meal would be a fitting intrusion unto such a sight! Forsooth! Doth my maiden stir?

*(***LYDIA*** sits up and looks around.)*

LYDIA. You know, normally I would freak out if I woke up with a man in my room giving an external monologue, but with you Fabio, it's just whatever.

FABIO. Thank you!

LYDIA. That wasn't a compliment. Get out.

FABIO. May I first say that thy hair, even unkempt with the wild attributes of bed-head, reminds me of seaweed floating in the deep?

LYDIA. You just did, so I guess so.

FABIO. Sweet Lydia, thy hair, even unkempt with the wild attributes of bed-head, still remind me of seaweed, floating softly in the waves!

LYDIA. Get out of my room. It's too early for this.

FABIO. As thy wish! Forsooth! But first, shan't thou try a morsel of the meal I have prepared for you?

LYDIA. Food!

FABIO. Indeed! Thou shalt find that I am a master chef, having learned from only the greatest in the land.

LYDIA. Except that Gretchen made this, right?

FABIO. Uh… No?

LYDIA. Really? Even though it's the same breakfast she always makes me? Speaking of which, where is she?

FABIO. Nowhere!

LYDIA. Fabio, you didn't kill her, did you?

FABIO. No! I merely ambushed her in the hall, and locked her in a closet.

LYDIA. Fabio!

FABIO. Lydia!

LYDIA. You can't keep doing things like that!

FABIO. Sure I can! See how fit I am?

*(**GRETCHEN** enters from out of nowhere again, preferably from the side of the stage that doesn't have a door.)*

GRETCHEN. Forsooth!

LYDIA. Gretchen! When did you get here!? Seriously!? Why is it that I *never* see you enter?

GRETCHEN. I do not mean to startle you, my lady. I am merely your humble maid Gretchen.

LYDIA. Well, how did you escape the closet Fabio locked you in?

GRETCHEN. Our closets don't have locks.

LYDIA. Oh. That actually makes sense.

FABIO. I probably should have been more thorough, but I was in such a rush to get to you, fair Lydia. I am sorry.

LYDIA. For ambushing her, or for not ambushing her well enough?

FABIO. Uh… Forsooth!

LYDIA. That's not an answer!

GRETCHEN. I think that it's the perfect answer!

LYDIA. Why are you taking his side on this? He just attacked you in the hallway!

FABIO. It was an assault in the name of love!

GRETCHEN. Perfectly justified.

LYDIA. Please, can you just leave me alone and let me eat my breakfast? I have a lot of stuff I need to do today.

FABIO. Forsooth! I shall help you!

LYDIA. Thank you Fabio, that's a noble thing for you to offer, but I think my business would go a little more smoothly without your... uh... "help."

FABIO. Aha! You jest most funnily, my well-fertilized morning flower! I meant help you eat your breakfast. All these ambushes really give a charming man such as myself quite an appetite!

LYDIA. Get out of my room!

FABIO. Never!

LYDIA. Hey, Gretchen, how about you go make Fabio some breakfast? I sure he would love that.

GRETCHEN. Forsooth! I am already gone!

(**GRETCHEN** *grabs* **FABIO** *by the arm and pulls him off stage.*)

FABIO. Forsooth! I will see you this afternoon!

(both exit)

LYDIA. I wonder if that was such a good idea, actually... Oh well, I'm sure they'll both be fine.

(lights down)

VII

(Lights up on the next scene. **LYDIA** *is back in the graveyard. It's foggy, and* **DAVIS** *is wearing a monk disguise.)*

LYDIA. Father Peter! Are you out here? The people in the chapel said that you usually like to walk around in the graveyard.

DAVIS. *(in a bad* **FATHER PETER** *impression)* Of course, I'm right over here. Come closer, my child, and tell me what is on your mind.

LYDIA. Well, you see, it has to do with my father's death. I understand you're a master of poison?

DAVIS (FATHER PETER). Of course. Here, let me show you what I have.

LYDIA. No, you misunderstand. I don't want to poison anyone.

DAVIS (FATHER PETER). Well, just step a little closer, and I'll tell you everything I know.

LYDIA. Why am I getting suspicious?

DAVIS. Because… Forget it. Don't move! This is a kidnapping!

*(***DAVIS*** pulls out a dagger and cackles evilly.)*

LYDIA. Oh, hi, Davis.

DAVIS. Don't even think about calling for help! We're alone in this graveyard!

LYDIA. How has everything been? Still plotting, I see.

DAVIS. At last! I have captured you! Muahaha!

LYDIA. Weird weather we're having, isn't it? The fog only seems to be in the graveyard.

DAVIS. Lydia, you don't really seem all that concerned.

LYDIA. I don't? Must be all of your previous failed attempts at evil.

*(***FATHER PETER** *enters.)*

PETER. Did I hear someone call my name?

LYDIA. Oh, there you are! Yes, I wanted to ask about my father's death.

DAVIS. Okay, seriously, people. I have a dagger and I *will* use it.

PETER. So much talk about death today. But then again, most of my days do seem to end up that way. With death. It's an inevitable topic of conversation, sort of like it is in life.

LYDIA. Okay… Should I come back later?

PETER. No. You can't just forget about it and expect something to have changed. The death's still there. Forsooth. Ask away.

LYDIA. Okay, so…

DAVIS. Stab!

LYDIA. I was thinking that –

DAVIS. Stabby stab!

LYDIA. Davis, could you stop interrupting our conversation? It's rude.

DAVIS. Aren't you listening to me? *I'm kidnapping you.*

LYDIA. That's rude too, come to think of it.

DAVIS. I'm serious! Stop ignoring me!

PETER. To be perfectly honest, my son, you do seem to be slightly inept at evil.

DAVIS. It's not my fault! She just keeps ruining things!

PETER. I'm sure she does. Lydia, how do these accusations make you feel?

LYDIA. Why are we talking about this again?

PETER. Forsooth. I'm a psychologist too.

LYDIA. Remind me never to visit you for any future depression.

PETER. Enough, Lydia. What are thy feelings on the matter?

LYDIA. Well… Davis just doesn't seem like that evil a person to me.

DAVIS. I am! I'm very evil!

PETER. What's the most evil thing you're ever done, Davis?

DAVIS. I once parked my carriage… in front of the town well!

PETER. Well, that's not so bad.

DAVIS. What if there had been a fire? The city could have burned down! Everyone could have died!

LYDIA. Okay, seriously, what's with all the foreshadowing!?

PETER. Lydia, please don't interrupt. I'm sure everyone would have been fine. Anything else, Davis?

DAVIS. I once killed a kitten!

LYDIA. What!?

DAVIS. That's right! I'm evil!

LYDIA. That doesn't sound like something you would do.

DAVIS. Well, maybe you just don't know me that well.

LYDIA. I'm not convinced.

DAVIS. Okay, maybe I just adopted a kitten.

LYDIA. Aha! I knew it!

DAVIS. You could at least respect me!

LYDIA. Why? So that you could try to mess things up with me and Fabio again? Oh wait, you're inept at that as well!

DAVIS. Oh, come on. You would *love* for something bad to happen between you and Fabio!

LYDIA. I don't know what you're talking about.

DAVIS. Oh, I think you do. You're just putting up with him because you think you have to! You don't even like him!

LYDIA. But I *do* have to put up with him! That's the thing! I'm sorry I've been ignoring you, but you don't have to start kidnapping people to get attention!

DAVIS. What else am I supposed to do? I'm the bad guy, remember?

LYDIA. Hardly!

DAVIS. Why's that?

LYDIA. Because you…

DAVIS. I'm waiting…

LYDIA. Well, you're too nice of a guy to be evil.

DAVIS. I don't see many other options available. If we can't be friends, we have to be enemies, so I'm kidnapping you. Like it or not.

LYDIA. Well I don't like it!

DAVIS. You don't?

LYDIA. No. I mean, I wish we could be friends, but I can't be friends with the bad guy.

DAVIS. I thought you just said I wasn't such a bad guy.

LYDIA. But you have to be! Who else would be the bad guy?

DAVIS. I don't know, maybe the person who *murdered your father?*

(awkward pause)

LYDIA. Oh. That makes sense.

DAVIS. Sure does.

(another awkward pause)

DAVIS. So… does that make us friends now?

LYDIA. I guess I could let you help me out with this. But just for a while.

DAVIS. Great! Where do we start?

PETER. Well, I recently sold some generic poison to Lady Morgan, but she said she just wanted it for rats. Then she laughed evilly. You might want to look into that.

LYDIA. Perfect. Let's go!

*(**LYDIA** and **DAVIS** exit. **FATHER PETER** stays on stage for a moment.)*

PETER. Forsooth, I must be the greatest psychologist ever!

*(**PETER** exits. Lights down.)*

VIII

(Lights up on the entrance to **LADY MORGAN**'s *hall, with the hall itself on the other side of the stage.* **DAVIS** *is standing back and looking up.)*

DAVIS. Well, this isn't intimidating at all. Just a murderer's mansion with messed-up masonry.

LYDIA. What, you don't like gargoyles?

DAVIS. Of course not! They're statues that look like they want to kill you. Do we really have to go in? This suddenly seems like a bad idea.

LYDIA. Do you have a better idea?

DAVIS. Yes. *Not this.* I swear, if this play were horror, this would be the stupid mistake that gets us killed. Can we bring the city guard or something?

LYDIA. We don't have any proof besides the fact that she bought rat poison. How bad could it be? If she decides to kill us, we could always just leave.

DAVIS. Lydia, don't you dare –

*(***LYDIA** *knocks on the door. They wait for a second, but nothing happens.)*

DAVIS. Well, looks like nobody's home. Let's leave.

(The door opens with a slow creak.)

LYDIA. Okay, fine, it's a little creepy, but I'm sure it's fine. Don't be such a baby.

DAVIS. It's a bad idea…

(As the two slowly enter, organ music starts playing. Lights up on the other side of the stage, where **LADY MORGAN** *sits in front of said organ, dressed in whatever clothing and a black cape.)*

DAVIS. You've got to be kidding me.

LYDIA. Uh, excuse me? Lady Morgan?

(**MORGAN** *stops playing and stands up, turning around to greet them. She has a Transylvanian accent.*)

MORGAN. Forsooth! Visitors! If it isn't dear Lydia, come to pay me a visit! Please, sit down, make yourselves comfortable.

LYDIA. Thank you Lady Morgan, but we actually came to ask you about something.

MORGAN. I don't go out during the day because I have sensitive skin. It burns quite easily.

LYDIA. Uh, no. That's not what I meant. There's something else.

MORGAN. The garlic? I have allergies!

DAVIS. I have the feeling that this conversation is going downhill fast.

MORGAN. What's that supposed to mean? You can't prove anything!

LYDIA. No, we just wanted to ask you about your meeting with Father Peter.

MORGAN. Ah, so thou hast been to see the monk about it, have you? Did he give thee holy water and stakes and tell you go kill me? I'll not have it!

(**MORGAN** *draws a sword, pointing it at* **LYDIA** *and* **DAVIS.**)

DAVIS. Now would be a good time to leave.

LYDIA. Yeah, sounds like it.

(*They run to the door, but can't seem to open it.*)

LYDIA. It's stuck!

MORGAN. Yes, it most certainly is! Forsooth! You have fallen into my trap, and now thou art doomed!

LYDIA. But I just wanted to know why you were buying –

MORGAN. The fresh blood?

LYDIA. What!?

MORGAN. Oh, you didn't know about that. Well, it doesn't matter! You already know too much!

LYDIA. Seriously!? I can't believe you've managed to keep things a secret for so long. We just walked in!

MORGAN. Oh. So you didn't notice anything strange about my behavior?

DAVIS. Well, did you poison Sir Harold?

MORGAN. Forsooth! I am such a fool! You thought me a mere murderer. No, I didn't use the poison to kill him, but to kill rats.

DAVIS. Oh yeah? Prove it! You're insane! Why should we believe you?

(**MORGAN** *pulls a dead rat out of a pocket.*)

MORGAN. What do you think *this* is!?

DAVIS. Okay, *now* you're crazy. Can we leave?

MORGAN. Forsooth, if only it were that simple! Thou hath heard too much! Though thy may not be able to put the pieces together, I shall tell thee my secret! I… am a vampire! And now… you must die!

LYDIA. This is the worst plot twist I've ever seen! Why the hell would anybody write this!?

MORGAN. Lydia, shouldn't you be panicking right now? Isn't complaining a little… *Out of character* for you?

(**MORGAN** *gives* **LYDIA** *"the stare."*)

LYDIA. Really? Even when you're about to kill us?

(**MORGAN** *continues "the stare."*)

LYDIA. Fine. Forsooth.

MORGAN. There is no escape! Any last words?

DAVIS. I'm sorry I tried to be evil!

LYDIA. I'm sorry I never gave you a chance!

DAVIS. I'm sorry I keep trying to break you and Fabio up!

LYDIA. I'm sorry I stole your coin purse on the way over here!

DAVIS. Wait, what?

MORGAN. And now, you die!

FABIO. *(offstage)* Forsooth!

MORGAN. What!?

> *(There's the sound of a window breaking, and* **FABIO** *leaps onto the stage, sword drawn.)*

FABIO. Die monster! You don't belong in this world!

LYDIA. Fabio!?

FABIO. My fairest Lydia! Art thou alright?

MORGAN. Forsooth! Not the legendary Fabio! His courage and rugged good looks spell my doom as surely as he can spell his own name!

FABIO. Ha! The joke's on you, vile leech! I can't spell in the slightest!

MORGAN. Oh no!

FABIO. Oh yes!

MORGAN. Then we shall engage in mortal combat!

FABIO. Forsooth!

> *(***FABIO*** stabs* **MORGAN**, *and she falls to the ground.)*

MORGAN. Fool! Don't you know that vampires can only be killed by a stake through the heart?

FABIO. No, I didn't! Thank you for telling me!

> *(***FABIO*** pulls a stake from out of nowhere and stabs* **MORGAN**.*)*

MORGAN. Forsooth! The heroic Fabio hath outsmarted me! Forsooth!

> *(***MORGAN*** dies.)*

DAVIS. Well, that was convenient.

LYDIA. Yup.

FABIO. Forsooth!

LYDIA. How exactly did you find us, Fabio? Or know we were in danger in the first place?

FABIO. It's a simple task for a mind as cunning and clever as my own.

LYDIA. That's not an answer.

FABIO. Forsooth!

LYDIA. You know what? Nevermind. Can we just get out of here and pretend this scene never happened?

FABIO. Of course not! There is one thing I must do first!

LYDIA. Which is…?

*(**FABIO** gets down on one knee.)*

FABIO. Fairest Lydia…

LYDIA. Oh God.

FABIO. Most rescuable damsel in all the land…

LYDIA. Is this the best place to do this? You did just kill someone.

FABIO. Yes, but out of love!

*(another of **GRETCHEN**'s out of nowhere entrances)*

GRETCHEN. He has a point!

LYDIA. What the hell!?

FABIO. Lydia, will you marry me?

LYDIA. Uh…

(long pause)

LYDIA. Can I get back to you on that?

FABIO. Of course you can! We have all the time in the world.

*(**FABIO** stands back up, but freezes as the lights flash and thunder rumbles. The **DIRECTOR** enters.)*

DIRECTOR. What have you been doing to my play!?

LYDIA. Oops.

(Lights dim as though it's the end of the scene.)

DIRECTOR. No you don't! I'll say when this scene is over!

(Lights come back on.)

DIRECTOR. I'm waiting for an answer.

LYDIA. I…it's just…he… Forsooth!

DIRECTOR. That doesn't work on me.

LYDIA. Dammit! What am I supposed to say!? I'm trying to go along with it, then you pull shit like *that*. What *was* that!?

DIRECTOR. Vampires sell. Mention a romance with vampires in it and you've instantly appealed to the entire female demographic.

LYDIA. You have no idea what you're talking about, do you?

DIRECTOR. That's for me to know, and you to find out.

LYDIA. Great. Can I go back to my part now?

DIRECTOR. Of course not! You can't turn Fabio down!

LYDIA. I didn't turn him down! I just…need more time.

DIRECTOR. More time, eh? I'll show you more time!

*(The **DIRECTOR** takes out a pen and starts scribbling on his clipboard.)*

LYDIA. What are you doing?

DIRECTOR. Making some much needed adjustments to the plot.

LYDIA. Thank God! You're removing that last scene?

DIRECTOR. You're welcome, and no, I'm not changing anything that's happened already. As a matter of fact, you should be happy to know that I'm taking a leaf out of your book.

LYDIA. What do you mean?

DIRECTOR. You've taught me something very important Lydia. You've taught me that sometimes…

*(The **DIRECTOR** finishes scribbling and looks up with an evilly sweet smile.)*

DIRECTOR. …You just need to improvise.

*(The **DIRECTOR** leaves the stage, and everything goes back to normal.)*

DAVIS. Gretchen, what are you doing here?

GRETCHEN. I've come to tell you something very important!

FABIO. Forsooth! What is it?

GRETCHEN. Sir Patrick, from the estate on the other side of town, has issued an ultimatum! He says that unless Lydia chooses someone to marry within two days, all her land and wealth is forfeit!

LYDIA. No!

FABIO. Yes!

DAVIS. Yes!

LYDIA. No!

FABIO. No?

DAVIS. Erm, no!

LYDIA. No! Yes!

FABIO. Yes?

LYDIA. Yes.

DAVIS. No!

LYDIA. No?

FABIO. No?

DAVIS. No! Yes!

LYDIA. Hold on, yes to the no?

DAVIS. No.

FABIO. Yes!

LYDIA. Maybe.

FABIO. Maybe?

LYDIA. Yes.

DAVIS. Will someone please tell me what's going on!?

GRETCHEN. I just did!

FABIO. Forsooth!

DAVIS. Shut up!

FABIO. Make me!

LYDIA. Woah, wait a second.

FABIO. Yes?

DAVIS. No!

GRETCHEN. Forsooth!

DAVIS. Well, I certainly hope you make a choice within two days, Lydia. I'll come by your estate later this evening. I have royal duties to take care of.

FABIO. And I'll be by your house at all times. Because I live there. I trust that you'll get back to me before time runs out. Forsooth!

DAVIS. Forsooth!

(**DAVIS** *and* **FABIO** *exit.*)

GRETCHEN. Forsooth mistress! It seems that your bold, brave Fabio has some competition from the rich noble Davis! But who will you choose?

(**LYDIA** *pauses, still not quite sure what just happened.*)

LYDIA. Um… Forsooth?

(lights down)

IX

(Lights up on **LYDIA***'s room.* **GRETCHEN** *enters, carrying a tea set.)*

GRETCHEN. Forsooth! Good 'morrow mistress! It is I, your humble maid Gretchen! Hath thou decided whom thou shalt wed yet?

LYDIA. No. Davis came by again yesterday, but he was pretty much focused on making himself look better then Fabio, so I made him leave. I didn't see Fabio at all yesterday, which is weird because he lives here, but I think he just forgot what was going on.

GRETCHEN. Forsooth! Thou shouldn't be so harsh on Fabio! He is surely the bravest –

LYDIA. That will be all, Gretchen.

GRETCHEN. But mistress!

LYDIA. But nothing. Uncle Laffy should be here soon, and I want his advice, not yours.

*(***GRETCHEN** *sets down the tea set, pouring the cups.)*

GRETCHEN. Very well mistress, I am but your humble maid, whose name is Gretchen.

LYDIA. I know your name! Just get out!

*(***GRETCHEN** *exits.* **LAFAYETTE** *enters.)*

LAFAYETTE. Forsooth, young Lydia! I understand that you have a difficult choice ahead of you tomorrow, no?

LYDIA. Yes, uncle! Unless I chose to marry either Fabio or Davis, Sir Patrick is going to take my land and wealth! What should I do?

LAFAYETTE. Hmm, I believe your best chance to get out of this situation is to get married.

LYDIA. Yes, I already figured that part out. But to who?

LAFAYETTE. To either Davis or Fabio.

LYDIA. Yes, I know that! You're not helping!

LAFAYETTE. Well, I reduced your options by about four billion people. Can't you take it from here?

LYDIA. Uncle Laffy!

LAFAYETTE. Yes?

LYDIA. Can't you just help me pick? I mean, I like Davis, but Fabio is so sweet. And Fabio's brave, while Davis really isn't. And Davis is smart, but Fabio is so incredibly stupid! How am I supposed to decide by tomorrow!?

LAFAYETTE. My dear young Lydia, the answer is simple. In these situations, you must simply listen to your heart.

LYDIA. That's not helpful at all!

LAFAYETTE. I know. When I try to listen to my heart, it just goes "Thumpa thumpa thumpa, look at me, I am a heart." Then I go "Heart! What should I do?" Then my heart goes "Shut up Lafayette! I am a heart!" Then I go "You shut up heart!" Then my heart goes "Okay!" Then I have a heart attack for a while, and when my heart finally starts again, I swear I can hear it laughing at me. Hearts can be asses, sometimes.

LYDIA. That's actually pretty good advice if you only listen to the last sentence. But I still don't know what I'm going to do!

LAFAYETTE. Don't worry Lydia, when I'm in your sort of situation, I always deal with it in the time honored tradition of arranging a spreadsheet with graphs on it.

LYDIA. A spreadsheet?

LAFAYETTE. With graphs on it, yes. I came prepared, and brought one with me.

LYDIA. Alright then, I guess it couldn't hurt to look at a few graphs.

LAFAYETTE. Excellent! We shall look at them right after tea.

LYDIA. Thanks for the help, Uncle Laffy! You have no idea how hard this has all been for me.

LAFAYETTE. You have a huge responsibility here, Lydia. I know that it can be stressful, but you must realize that whoever you marry will be put in charge of your estate, and will manage the rest of the village. Everyone is counting on your decision. No pressure.

(**LAFAYETTE** *picks up a cup and takes a sip.* **LYDIA** *picks up a cup as well, but* **LAFAYETTE** *knocks it out of her hands.*)

LYDIA. What the hell?

LAFAYETTE. Forsooth! Lydia! This tea is poisoned! More then usual, I mean! It has generic poison in it!

LYDIA. What? But this tea came from my house! It shouldn't have any poison in it at all!

LAFAYETTE. Au contraire, Lydia. It has at least seven different types of poison in it. All of them in highly lethal doses.

LYDIA. But who could have done this? This tea was brought straight here after it was made for me by –

(**GRETCHEN** *enters.*)

GRETCHEN. Your humble maid, Gretchen!

(**LAFAYETTE** *draws his sword.*)

LAFAYETTE. Stay behind me, Lydia! I shall keep you safe!

LYDIA. Gretchen!? I don't understand. Why would you do something like this?

GRETCHEN. Fabio deserves better then you! You're only marrying him because you have to! You don't love him the way I do!

LYDIA. This was unexpected... Wait, did you kill my father, too?

GRETCHEN. Forsooth! Perhaps your humble maid is less humble then you might have thought!

LYDIA. Wait, we don't have to fight! I might not even marry Fabio at all!

GRETCHEN. He loves you and you would turn your back on him!? I'll just have to kill you the old fashioned way!

LAFAYETTE. Please, do not even attempt it, psycho maid, or I shall be forced to harm you bodily with my weapon. You aren't even armed!

(**GRETCHEN** *jumps toward* **LAFAYETTE**, *who swings at her. She ducks, and punches him in the gut.* **LAFAYETTE** *falls to the ground, unconscious.*)

LYDIA. What the hell!? He was a trained bodyguard!

GRETCHEN. That's where you have underestimated me! Before I came here to be your maid, I was trained in subtle art of ninjutsu!

LYDIA. You're a freaking ninja!? How is that supposed to make any sense!?

GRETCHEN. Your father was very concerned for your safety. I was a secret bodyguard the entire time!

LYDIA. How's that job working out for you? You're trying to kill me.

GRETCHEN. Forsooth! Ha ha ha!

LYDIA. You're crazy! Besides, any minute now Fabio is going to come running through that door. He always does.

GRETCHEN. You think I haven't thought of that!? I locked him in the hall closet!

LYDIA. Those don't have locks, remember?

GRETCHEN. Try telling that to Fabio. He's been stuck in it for twelve hours now.

LYDIA. Shit.

(**DAVIS** *enters.*)

DAVIS. Lydia, I was just… What's going on here?

GRETCHEN. I WILL KILL EVERYONE WITH MY BARE HANDS!

DAVIS. Oh, I see. I'll just be leaving then.

LYDIA. Davis! Help!

DAVIS. Sorry, ninjas are not something I like to deal with.

(**DAVIS** *exits, and* **GRETCHEN** *turns to* **LYDIA**.)

LYDIA. Davis?… Davis!

GRETCHEN. Davis cannot save you now!

*(**DAVIS** sneaks back on stage, holding a vase. He slowly sneaks toward **GRETCHEN**.)*

LYDIA. Forsooth, you are right! If only I had been better suited to Fabio's devotion! Truly, thou art party to only the most righteous of causes, as myself, the undeserving shrew, deserves nothing better then to– NOW, DAVIS!

*(**DAVIS** hits **GRETCHEN** over the head, and she falls to the floor.)*

LYDIA. Davis! That was… almost brave!

DAVIS. Thanks, I guess. Is Lafayette alright?

LYDIA. I'm sure he'll be fine.

LAFAYETTE. I can't feel my spleen!

LYDIA. Walk it off, uncle!

LAFAYETTE. But it hurts!

LYDIA. So, Davis… are you feeling up to a wedding tomorrow?

LAFAYETTE. But what about my spreadsheets?

DAVIS. Yes, Lydia, I would love a wedding.

(They embrace. Lights down.)

X

*(Lights up on the final scene. Various guests sit in various chairs, waiting for the wedding, while **FATHER PETER** prepares for the marrying part. **LYDIA** stands nervously off to one side. **FABIO** approaches.)*

LYDIA. Oh, Fabio. I wasn't sure if I was going to see you here.

FABIO. Forsooth! Where else would I be on such a glorious day? I can't wait for the wedding!

LYDIA. Fabio… You do know that I'm not marrying you, right?

FABIO. Of course I do! I'm not stupid.

LYDIA. Some would argue…

FABIO. Sorry, what was that?

LYDIA. Oh, I said "None would argue."

FABIO. Forsooth!

LYDIA. Fabio, I've been meaning to ask you… You're not mad at me or anything, are you? For choosing Davis?

FABIO. How can I be? It's your decision.

LYDIA. Well, yes, but the director wrote the play to be about true love. Surely that has some side effect when it doesn't work out?

FABIO. My dear deluded Lydia. That's not what true love is. True love is when you care about another person's happiness more then anything else in the world, including your own. If you want to marry Davis, and if it will make you happy, then that's good enough for me. Besides, it's not like you're going to fire me or anything, right?

LYDIA. Of course not Fabio! I wouldn't dream of it! Now go sit down, the wedding is about to start!

(FABIO sits, and LYDIA takes her place up beside FATHER PETER. DAVIS walks down the aisle to the tune of "here comes the bride.")

PETER. We are gathered here today to celebrate the marriage, and eventual death of two very rich people. Not that their money is going to help them when they're dead. If anyone has good reason these two should not be married, speak now or hold your piece until the day you die.

(The DIRECTOR stands up from where he was sitting.)

DIRECTOR. Not so fast!

(gasps abound)

LYDIA. Is that… the Director!?

DAVIS. No, that's Sir Patrick, the one who was going to steal your land and wealth.

LYDIA. Oh. Of course it is. Sir Patrick, I should have guessed that you would try and ruin my wedding. What is it this time?

DIRECTOR. You've ruined everything! You were supposed to pick Fabio, not Davis! Now, you shall suffer for this!

(The DIRECTOR draws a pen and readies his clipboard.)

DIRECTOR. Any last words?

LYDIA. Uh… Forsooth?

(FABIO jumps up, stabbing the DIRECTOR in the back.)

FABIO. Edit in hell, sorcerer! Forsooth!

(The DIRECTOR falls to the ground.)

DIRECTOR. Forsooth, Fabio! I am… Your father! Gaaaaaaahhhhhh…

(The DIRECTOR dies.)

FABIO. NOOOOOOOO!!!

(FABIO sits back down calmly.)

FABIO. Now that that's over with, I believe we have a wedding?

PETER. Forsooth. Lydia, do you take Davis to be your lawfully wedded husband, 'til death do you part?

LYDIA. I…

(**LYDIA** *looks at* **FABIO**, *then back to* **DAVIS**.)

LYDIA. I do.

PETER. Davis, same question?

DAVIS. I most certainly do!

PETER. I now pronounce you man and wife! You may kiss the bride.

(They kiss, applause. They bow, and lights dim.)

DAVIS. Ha ha ha…

(Lights come back up. Everyone is staring at **DAVIS**.*)*

DAVIS. Ha ha ha ha ha… AH HAHAHAHAHAHA!!! MUAHAHAAHAAA!!!

LYDIA. Uh, Davis sweetie, is something wrong?

DAVIS. You fools! You've fallen directly into my trap!

LYDIA. You've got to be kidding me…

DAVIS. It's all mine! The power! The riches! Nothing can stop me now! Effective immediately, I am doubling all taxes! Anyone who cannot meet these new standards will be executed! All who oppose me shall fall! First, the fiefdom, next, the kingdom, then, THE WORLD! HAHAHAHAHAH!!!

LYDIA. You married me for power!?

DAVIS. Of course I did! I told you as much when I met you, didn't I!? And you all fell for it! Oh, look at Davis, he used to be the villain, but now he's trying to turn over a new leaf. OR IS HE!? HAHAHAHAHAHA!

LYDIA. You'll never get away with this! Guards, arrest him!

DAVIS. Nobody is going to help you anymore, Lydia! By our sacred law, they now owe their lives and allegiances to me! None would dare break this law, not even loyal Lafayette! I've won! Gretchen, get out here!

*(***GRETCHEN*** enters.)*

LYDIA. I thought you were locked in the dungeon?

GRETCHEN. Master Davis let me out.

DAVIS. You see, she's been working for me the entire time! I didn't poison you father myself, I just had Gretchen do it.

LYDIA. You son of a bitch!

DAVIS. And what are you going to do about it? The entire town is on my side!

FABIO. Or are they!? Forsooth!

*(**FABIO** jumps up and draws his sword.)*

DAVIS. Really? Is this all you've got? One lone servant who doesn't understand what just happened?

FABIO. It looks like you're going to need more men!

DAVIS. And he can't count odds either! Townsfolk! Kill him!

FABIO. Over here, Lydia! I'll protect you!

*(Everyone at the wedding stands up and draws a sword. The stage is now divided, with **FABIO** and **LYDIA** on one side, and the rest of the cast, on the other.)*

FABIO. Hang on, what's Sir Harold doing over there?

LYDIA. Father! What the hell!?

HAROLD. You see Lydia, I am a vampire now! I owe allegiance to Davis, as the undead cannot rule!

LYDIA. And I thought Lady Morgan was dead too!

FABIO. Die monster, you don't belong in this world!

MORGAN. It is not by my own hand that I am once again given flesh. I was called here by humans who wished to pay me tribute!

FABIO. Tribute!? You steal men's souls, and make them your slaves!

MORGAN. Perhaps the same could be said of all religions!

LYDIA. You guys realize that nobody in the audience understands what pop culture reference you're making, right?

FABIO. Maybe we should stick with Twilight.

DAVIS. Shut up! Clever wordplay won't save you now! ATTACK!

(lights down)

XI

(End of the final scene: lights up. The entire cast, with the exception of **LYDIA**, **FABIO**, *and* **DAVIS** *lie dead on the stage, in various overdramatic death poses, dressed in Shakespearian clothing.* **FABIO** *stands in a dramatic pose next to* **LYDIA**, *while* **DAVIS** *hides badly behind an overturned prop.)*

FABIO. Alas, my fair Lydia, that it has come to this. For here lie dead on this field of most unfortunate battle everyone we have ever known. The entire village is destroyed, and now, we must make our own fortunes in the far away lands known as Beverly Hills. If only my father were here to see this!

LYDIA. Yes, dear Fabio, but you killed him not five minutes ago.

FABIO. Alas! 'Tis true! 'Tis a sad day, and to think that the one responsible remains as of yet at large.

*(***DAVIS*** cackles evilly.)*

FABIO. Forsooth! What doth this cackling portray?

*(***DAVIS*** jumps out from behind the barrel, holding a very small dagger.)*

DAVIS. This shall be the end of you, valiant hero! En Guard!

*(***FABIO*** stabs ***DAVIS***, who dies overdramatically.)*

FABIO. Alas! The day is won!

LYDIA. 'Tis true! Thou hath saved the day, Fabio. Forsooth!

(They embrace, and the lights go down again. Lights come back up, spotlight on **LYDIA**, *holding a dictionary.)*

LYDIA. Forsooth: adverb. One: Indeed. Often used ironically or to express surprise or indignation. Two:

Used to give an ironic politeness to questions. How it ended up becoming a play, I'll never know.

(lights down)

End of Play

www.ingramcontent.com/pod-product-compliance
Lightning Source LLC
Chambersburg PA
CBHW071412290426
44108CB00014B/1791